salmonpoetry40

Publishing Irish & International Poetry Since 1981

The Forgetting and Remembering of Air *is a stunning piece of work — an achingly moving narrative of love for a child, parent, sibling, lover or icon. In these poems Hubbard is travelling through love and its possibilities of home, moving fast towards the acceptance of the disappointment, the ruin of it, like that great house of the cover.*

THE NEW WELSH REVIEW

There is nothing safely aesthetic about these poems, beautifully observed though they frequently are. The watching intelligence reaches so far into the places, situations or works of art that it nearly forgets itself, and maybe desires to. The central block of poems on the tragic deaths of women signal that danger, and make it all the more of an achievement when the closing poems journey to the edge of the Atlantic, almost beyond comfort or habitable land, and come back with a final, hard-won '...yes'.

PHILIP GROSS

'There are two kinds of islands' begins the poem, 'Dreaming of Islands', 'those born of erasure and fracture'. From the 'river's dark skin' at Bow Creek to Yves Klein, from St Ives to Prussian Blue; from Cliff and Elvis to Charing Cross, from Dora Carrington to Diane Arbus, Sue Hubbard locates places and people with a lyrical precision of voice, following those erasures and fractures to a 'fragile yes'. The poems surge with a natural force breathing the world 'into and out of itself'. A mixture of nature and art; this is an impressive book.

GEORGE SZIRTES

Whether describing the Thames estuary or the remote west coast of Ireland, Sue Hubbard pays close and exact attention to the elemental world and the vulnerability of the human within it. These moving poems face the 'anthracite dark' outside and inside us, and emerge renewed by it, like prayers 'written on the waves'.

PASCALE PETIT

Swimming to Albania
Sue Hubbard

Published in 2021 by
Salmon Poetry
Cliffs of Moher, County Clare, Ireland
Website: www.salmonpoetry.com
Email: info@salmonpoetry.com

ISBN 978-1-912561-06-3

Cover Image:
'Peel Sound — Sunset.' Barbara Rae CBE, RA, RSA, RE

Cover Design & Typesetting: *Siobhán Hutson Jeanotte*

Printed in Ireland by Sprint Print

Salmon Poetry gratefully acknowledges the support of
The Arts Council / An Chomhairle Ealaíon

for my grandchildren

Acknowledgements

Versions of these poems first appeared in *The London Magazine, the Poetry Archive, The International Literary Quarterly, The Interpreters House, Ink, Sweat and Tears, Acumen, the Punch, 3 Quarks Daily, The Open Mouse, And Other Poems, Autumn Voices*, and the *Be Not Afraid* anthology in appreciation of Seamus Heaney. 'Remembering Laugharne' was commissioned by the artist Dan Llywelyn Hall for a Centenary Dinner for Dylan Thomas. 'Those Far Blue Hills' was published on the Manchester Metropolitan poetry website for poems written during lockdown, chosen by Carol Ann Duffy.

Special thanks are due to Stephen Duncan for his persistent encouragement, to Ruth Valentine, Deborah Alma, Martyn Crucefix, Annie Wilson and Linda Rose Parkes for their suggestions and help, to The Siena Art Institute, Cill Rialaig Artists Retreat, The Tyrone Guthrie Centre, Annaghmakerrig and the Bread Matters residency, Barreiro, Lisbon that all provided space to think and write.

Contents

1.

Lost in Space   11

1955, perhaps?   12

June   14

Snow   15

Silver Service   17

And soon...   18

Hats   19

So, what did you want from me, daddy?   20

Dog Days   21

Clissold Park   22

Churchyard   24

Firelight   25

Airman   26

Weather Forecast   27

Inheritance   28

Spring and Fall   29

2.

one thing   31

nuptials   33

Blood   34

face   35

another side of desire   36

Earth-Dreams   37

You   39

Visitor   40

Hare-witch   41

all morning   42

The Story of Silence   43

It's like this   44

Stigmata   45

Flying Ducks   46

Lake   47

Last Look   48

Return   49

Remembering Laugharne   50

3.

Lost   55

Afternoon in Siena   56

Reading the City   57

The Weight of History   58

Santa Maria della Scala   59

Sanctuary House of St. Catherine of Siena   60

Bar   61

A search for lightness against the weight of living   62

Vanishing Point   63

Fishers of Men   64

Duccio's Dawn   65

Barreiro   66

Travelling Alone   67

Night Square   68

Narrative Grace   69

Remembering Pessoa   70

Not Simply Air   71

Swimming to Albania   72

Those Far Blue Hills   73

About the Author   74

I

Of what is past, or passing, or to come.
W.B. Yeats

Lost in Space

There are galaxies inside me,
interstellar stars and dust.
I am full of dark matter,
quarks and spirals
of deep love that cannot
be seen with the naked eye,
lives that might have been
different under other alignments.
Somewhere amid black holes
and the absorption of light,
beyond the mass of Milky Way,
there's a distant room:
the walls covered with faded flowers,
a meadow of flecked sunlight,
where a child lies beneath
a bleached quilt in a narrow bed
dreaming of a boat
with a single blue sail,
a boat that will take her home.

1955, perhaps?

Late winter afternoon. A London Park.
The distant trees ghostly on the far
bank of the bleak lake.
Four and seven, say, in camel coats
with beaver collars, feeding the ducks.
I am holding a bag of bread
standing beside my sister
as we stare ahead in the line of duty
with nothing between us except
a strip of grey water
and a single moorhen sailing blithely by.
Above rain clouds gather
as the last few birds dart for shelter
before the sky splits open.

June

You stand in the scuffed Box Brownie square,
pretty and slim in your summer shorts,
your Hedy Lemarr hair, in front of a stage-left
parasol somewhere on the Côte d'Azure,
between your two young daughters
like the border guard between rival nations.
All of us squinting in the unfamiliar sun.

The past is another country,
one I barely remember as I search
our eyes to understand the real story.
I forget what was going on in front of us.
A man waving to his wife from the sea?
A barefoot boy in a sombrero
selling sugared almonds on the beach?
Children in a pedalo, laughing?

Years later, as you lie trying to catch
your shallow breath in the summer heat,
the same month as your name,
the same month as your birth,
I sit beside your cot holding
your frail hand in mine —
like a child in danger of getting lost —
wanting to tell you: this is who I am,
this has been the story,
that there are no drafts,
no proofs to be corrected,
that we don't get to write it again.

Snow

Lost in an infinity of misted mirrors,
among shelves of Optrex,

Pepsodent and pink calamine,
I dunked net petticoats into sugar solution

to froth out the nylon frills
of that first dance dress.

Hanging it to drip-dry over
the porcelain sink I squeezed

obdurate adolescent flesh
into a rubber roll-on

that chafed my thighs,
attached 15 deniers to silk suspenders,

before turning to straighten
the wayward seam along

a newly shaved leg and wriggling
into my strapless Wonderbra.

Then, spitting into the little
Bakelite box to soften the black wax,

a flick of mascara
applied with the tiny brush.

Backcombing my hair, the lady
on the tin of Elnett hairspray

smiled with a poise
I knew I could never muster.

So much preparation
to end alone

beneath the rotating mirror ball,
as the last waltz faded

and flakes of light spangled
my bare arms in falling snow.

Silver Service

Why should I remember,
after fifty years, that thirteen-year-old

crushed among the putrid hotel bins
behind the steamy kitchen door,

a meaty odour of gravy seeping
from his acned skin.

How little I knew as his wet tongue
slithered between my untutored lips,

his bitten fingers searched for the hooks
along my cotton schoolgirl bra.

I hardly knew whether the terror
of detection or the growing hardness

inside his waiter's trousers,
pressed against my yellow summer dress,

frightened me more. Was this love,
I wondered? Upstairs in the mirrored

dining room a tuxedoed band
was playing 'Fools Rush In',

while my parents waited
for silver service.

And soon...

           soon, it will be over,
the voyage's end coming into sight
like a bright spit of unmapped land,

as the old yawl turns slowly back into harbour
with its arbour of rusty fish sheds
shrouded in late evening fog.

The saffron light of portholes already dimmed,
the tattered sails lowered,
halyard and spinnakers stilled and trimmed,

furled jibs lashed against the mast.
A sea away I wait on this Atlantic headland
where icy galaxies keep me company in the dark

and a dogfox barks in a high wet field.
While in those far off Surrey hills
you falter and wane, so I wish my childhood songs

had not been mined in dust and pain,
those black diamonds of hurt and absence.
And now, when all that's unspoken

is cinders on my tongue, I want to call out:
daddy, oh my daddy, I've been here all along,
waiting across this cold violet sea.

Hats

The tallboy's empty now except
for your hats: three battered panamas
trimmed with striped Petersham bands
squatting in the mahogany dark.
One a jaunty fedora, the sort worn by
a Cuban paterfamilias with hairy arms,
sporting a large Havana cigar.
The other more elegant,
with a wide brim and a Mafioso air
that would be at home on a terrace
above the sparkling bay of Naples,
with a plate of *frutti di mare*
and a carafe of local wine,
or on the bald pate of an oncologist
watching his young mistress
slowly tanning in the sun.
The third, the most battered,
with a hole in the crown,
is the one you wore to deadhead
the roses in your rust-coloured
chinos and old cashmere,
before settling with that glass
of G&T as the sun went down.
Now, as afternoon fades
into evening, the deep wardrobe
radiates its own particular light,
and there's silence everywhere.

So, what did you want from me, daddy?

As you lay dying across a sea
and rain clouds rolled in between

that margin of ocean and sky,
where light is naked,

I lay on that narrow bed
figuring out how to get home.

The fate of our lives is the fate
of our wounded courage.

The road I've taken
ends only in another road.

Midsummer and the evening
is long, the rain clouds cleared.

A blood-red sun sinks
below the horizon and I wonder

what would've made you
take that small girl

in your arms and hug her
against your tobacco chest?

What was it you wanted, daddy,
from your first-born child?

Dog Days

Summer slips away, the light chrysanthemum,
the last nasturtiums blousy among the exhausted greens.
Sage and lemon balm wither against the stained brick wall
and in the quiet room, where charcoal light hunkers
among hairballs and dust, the mirror's lustre dims
as I lay my unread book beside the dish of lavender.

It's six months now, and I think of you more often
than when you were living: sitting in that striped deckchair
beside the laurel hedge, your battered panama
shading your eyes, your white beard
a bit rabbinical — though neatly trimmed — a glass of single malt
raised in a playful toast.

At my desk, wearing your old, checked shirt,
I follow this thread back among sulphurous shadows,
through the scent of rust and roses, till your voice,
patrician, acerbic, affectionate drifts through the open door,
filling the mauve twilight like blown leaves,
or those itinerant generations lost in the gathering dusk.

Clissold Park

Croo-croo! Croo-croo!
An invisible wood pigeon calls

from the far fringe of trees,
his fat-bodied song stuffed full of early summer.

Ad infinitum he repeats himself,
pausing only for echoes.

These city's greens are deceptive
of a certain peace. Lovers sprawl

on fresh mown grass.
Toddlers giggle smeared in ice cream.

And with the bird's insistent refrain
I'm back in that Surrey rose-garden

where grief, though present,
is still only a dream.

How quickly a month slips by —
that hiatus between a breath and a breath —

when your paper hand still held
some feeble warmth.

Ticking off each fragile gasp,
a minute is enough to know a life,

the dead impervious
to our childhood questions,

the truth a void they can no longer fill.
And now, you have no need of birdsong.

But oh, that I'd spoken of what was lodged
in this pigeon heart. Taken a chance,

before you walked off into the night,
choosing not to look back. Afraid.

Churchyard

Maybe this wind knows
something we don't, daddy,
   a secret it hugs close
and won't share
as it blows across
   the village churchyard
and the vicar firms the edge
of the freshly dug hole
   with her wellington boot,
opens the labelled canister
and tips you in.
   It's the plastic Evian bottle
that throws me, with which
she rinses the caddy,
   swirling round the water
to make sure she has every
last speck, every particle
   of ash that was you.

Firelight

No stars tonight.
Just sea and rain-soaked silence.
I've lit the stove,

poured the cut-price wine.
It's when you least expect
them they appear,

the unsolicited shadows of the dead,
the young man I never knew
until he became my father.

A few days ago, I found
a photograph foxed and faded
in black and white, a war-time airman

with the look of my son.
Leather brief case, gloves,
winged cap and something

uncertain about the eyes —
among the cocked hats, the brass buttons,
of his squadron

now all done with the novellas of their lives.
Brothers, husbands, accountants,
butchers, poets...

they scatter their days
like children kicking up leaves,
so, if I listen carefully

in this fire-lit hush, I can hear them
marching down the wooded path
into the torrential rain.

Airman

Somewhere on the other side of evening,
where the weather hangs heavy
in the darkening sky,

I search for you in the firelight
as the room turns its face to the past.
I can't tell the year,

though you're young,
dressed in flying gear, looking upwards
at something

beyond the camera's edge
with a touch of Kenneth More, say,
in *Reach for the Sky*.

Though I look for you
in the present tense, you remain
obdurate in black and white.

Your life ahead — a choice of wives.
Three, as yet, unnamed children.
How do I make sense of dust,

insubstantial as the shadows
on these whitewashed walls?
What alchemy

might give you substance,
invest this space with
all that was you

as evening lengthens,
and I collide with your absence,
with all that was never said?

Weather Forecast

shape-shifting mists
fluid as memory
dissolve the horizon
morning tides turn
beneath a fugitive sun
from whale-grey to yellow
to malachite green
last time I was here
you lay dying
across the Irish sea
as a cold wind blew in
from the derelict islands —
though the world
remains illegible
the fog peels back
and everything is
transparent —
a hole in the clouds
lets in the rain
so I can see right
through you to the sky

Inheritance

They cannot love me,
this painting of a small girl

in a dirty white dress
dwarfed by the rough stone walls

of a stinking Parisian yard,
or the hand-painted Italian *chiffonier*

where my father kept the Sunday squares
of Cadbury's Dairy Milk

in its purple foil wrapper,
or the gilded shell-shaped stool

where he threw his paisley bathrobe
as he stood before the mirror to shave.

They cannot take me in their arms,
approve of what was never

approved of amongst the living.
And though I've always dreaded absence,

they're mute now. For life hinges
on presence and affection.

In the pale morning light I run
my fingers over them

just one more time. Scoop up
the last crumbs of love.

Then let them go.

Spring and Fall

After Gerard Manley Hopkins

And so it goes on, this grieving
like a shadow of dark feathers leaving
a veil to cover the memory of you,
as slowly I am forgetting the essential you:
the essence, the hue, as I grow older
and my heart shrinks and grows colder
so by and by, with resigned and painful sigh
I come to accept, what of course, is a lie
that there are answers to my eternal why.
No matter, now, what name
I use, the sorrow remains the same —
an unvoiced love forever unexpressed:
what faint heart yearned for, what ghost guessed,
that blight no child should be born for,
and you the father I still mourn for.

II

My past is everything I failed to be.
Fernando Pessoa

one thing

has always mattered:
not to sit quietly in the shadows
of an evening room
with a glass of beaded water
and a newly sharpened pencil
waiting in case a butterfly or moth
happens to fly in — a Feathered Thorn
or Scalloped Oak, perhaps,
or on a good day a Scarlet Tiger —
its black and white wings
flashed with orange,
demanding to be in a poem.
Nor to walk in the freshness
of morning watching the swans,
who know nothing of divorce,
dive heads–down–tails–up
for frogs and molluscs,
or lie in new mown grass,
skirt pulled up to sun
my winter–white legs,
nor stand, here, on the edge
of the wild Atlantic
watching as a winding sheet of mist
rolls in, but to wake
mirrored in another's gaze:
its unplumbed depths.

nuptials

I have waited too long in this
astringent world
so cut petticoats
of lace from the white surf
stitched sequins of sunlight onto
the muslin of morning
caught with
a girdle of willow about my waist
placed a crown of terns' feathers
in my wild hair
plaited a sea grass ring
and given it to myself
before cutting up the sky
to sprinkle its blue fragments
over the high cliffs like
confetti

Blood

Still I carry the memory of that acrid reek —
metallic as those copper ha'pennies collected

in a cracked Coronation jar beside my bed —
which once oozed through these, now,

barren lands where the earth's pliant skin
has puckered into fissures, the pull

of those spring tides when lunar light
regulated the flow of the body electric,

each month the endometrium thickening
to the promise of what might be born.

When I dipped a finger into
that last shedding it tasted of loss.

Outside, the city curls foetal
beneath its sodium quilt while I listen

to the blip–blip of this tired heart
folding back into its crone body,

the expectant moon full and milky
nestled over the neighbour's chimney.

face

who is that young women over there
half-hidden behind a mask   bubbles
of saliva coating her dry lips   little hairs
sprouting from her chin thinking
she's still the person she's meant to be
why is she stitching her skin
into neat pleats and pouches to tuck
discretely behind her ears so no one
can see her thin mouth sutured with   fear
the smell of age on her like the stinking breath
of a dog   the pelt between her crotch
going bald
       dis-gust-ing
who would want to touch something
so dirty   so broken   puddle their fingers
in those dried up holes   that patch of psoriasis
better turn a blind eye   tell her to take off
that ridiculous disguise   it's a silly game anyway
       e -m -b -a -r-r -a -s-s -i -n -g
pull back the curtain   wipe up the spilt pee
show some decorum   some
       con-sid-er-a-tion
that's quite enough now

another side of desire

march–morning
   and out towards the islands the strait
is burnished with pewter highlights
   the stale language of beauty
sucking up all the words to describe
   what nevertheless is true
it concentrates the mind
   all this expansive loveliness
in contrast to the loss of small things
   the conspiracy of 2
that sets the world on fire
   the urgency of that midnight kiss
the tangled sheets of desire
   those loves that do not appear
the *l o n g i n g*
   for what might have been
in a space without gravity
   there's no weight
so I listen for the skylark
   singing in the high wide blue

Earth-Dreams

But a mermaid has no tears
and, therefore, suffers so much more.

HANS CHRISTIAN ANDERSEN

All night I dreamt of land. Of soil
crumbling through my fingers to leave
black parings under broken nails,

of fields spread with dung and that melancholy
light of autumn, the colours of clay and fire,
where morning has a yellow tongue.

Could I exist in air?
In this oceanic deep you lie embedded
in the womb of my heart,

attached by an umbilicus of longing,
my aqueous nightgown transparent
as air.

I don't even know who this you is.
Though I've pictured your all too human body
naked on my bed of cowrie shells,

visualised our house of cloth and tar,
ash walls mortared with the glue
of boiled fish bones.

Water accepts everything,
even the misshapen.
Over and over I've tried to imagine

a need for balance,
that slow steadying of the inner ear,
metatarsals pushing into solid ground.

Yet though I wait and wait
time returns me only to myself
as night to morning,

as sea to the shore,
but where your voice
should be, there is only silence.

You

There you are again at the far end of the empty beach,
scrambling over rocks beneath the abandoned nunnery

painted ice-cream green. Fleet as a greyhound,
tiny as a mote floating in the outer corner of my eye,

matted hair a billowing ghost of rain as the day
folds back into its rookery of clouds.

I've caught a glimpse of you before:
a shadow on the wall of empty streets

where silence sounds like noise. Barely noticed,
you stand among stagnant puddles

by the graffiti-etched door in a pool of winter light.
You bear a name you did not ask for,

trace the history of longing in your veins,
your lost passions in the March wind.

At night you are salt and ash. A low scream
trapped in the foxed mirror of the moon.

Visitor

New Year's Day and a poem
is prowling outside in the sleet
and high wind. I can sense him
hunched under the eaves
of the stone cottage,
down on the edge of the cliff
where sheep stand huddled
among bog and gorse
above the churning surf,
collar pulled up against the rain
dripping from the rim of his wide hat.
Maybe he's just sailed in
across the Atlantic hauling
an alphabet bag up the beach
like a smuggler's hoard,
along with a trunk of diphthongs
for ballast, nearly thrown
overboard into the rough sea.
I'm considering asking him in
to take shelter but am uncertain.
After all I've no idea where
he's from. What he might say.

Hare-witch

She knows every
boggy nook, each
clump of gorse
and reed, can pinpoint
Orion's Belt hanging
over the headland,
the star-fog
of the Milky Way,
translate the heaving
waves, the sleet gales
and rumble of distant thunder,
predict the neap tides
of a waning moon.
Trapped by the car's beam
she stops stock still.
Her frightened eyes,
her cleaved mouth
twitching in wet fur.
That familiar face
staring back at me from
the measureless dark.

all morning

I watch the suck and swell
of a single wave
grey-green and lamp-black
skittering and splitting
against this rock
veined with iron memories
a vortex of water-patterns
mingling with rain
twists and skeins
flashing like a juggler's
newly-sharpened knives
bubbles spurting
from the granite blow-hole
the world is a bowl of water
everything in flux
earth-dweller that I am
I stand on this lip
of land the wind
tugging my hair
the tide rehearsing
its old arguments
so when nothing else is left
there's still the movement
of this moment and
this wave conjugating
the fragile present

The Story of Silence

Because it has not turned out how I dreamt,
to lie against another's backbone in the dark

listening to the suck and blow of their dolphin breath,
I return to the edge of sea, sky and land,

where dawn is washed by rain-soaked night
to reveal a tattered wedding veil of mist

covering the morning's face.
Far from the city's buzz and blur,

the constant ticker tape of news,
I am postulant to the weather-god,

genuflect to the pull of tides,
whisper rosaries to a glassy moon,

the great Atlantic storms.
At break of day I light a beeswax candle

so solitude becomes a form
of holy erudition,

the I an Eye, before I merge
with this savage silence.

It's like this

or nearly —
  for everything is simply

an approximation, a wavering,
  a tentative reaching towards, what?

that journey of self-in-search-of-the-self
  those breaking waves, for example,

climbing that hill of glistening shingle
  relentless as Sisyphus,

only to fall back and do it all
  againandagainandagain

with a wh-oo-sh,
  a l–o–n–g s–l–o–w e — x — h — a — l — e

of sucking pebbles — why?
  because movement is the tide's essence —

like that blackbird outside
  my city window

whose language of high notes
  breaks the urban silence —

not in the hope of dawn or lightness —
  but because dragging phrases

from its little feathered breast
  is what it does

so, tell yourself overandover,
  until you believe it,

that you don't regret growing old,
  that it's part of the process,

the exploration, like twilight
  collecting in the deep stairwell

or dry leaves
  drifting in the gathering dark

Stigmata

Out walking at dawn,
the early morning spreads
like hope new-born
across the pewter lake.
In the deep hush
all is possibility,
the sun rising to burnish
the deep dark water,
but pushing through the dense
summer undergrowth,
I lose the narrow path
and slash my leg on briars
so blackberries of blood
gather in a bright-beaded anklet.

Flying Ducks

I keep attempting to reach the lake
but all the paths double back
before they get to the edge,
or disappear in clumps
of cleg-infested bracken.
I try again down another track,
fringed pink with rosebay willow
turning fast to end-of-summer
beards but am thwarted
by a scribble of briars.
I can see it through the trees,
the verticals of tall dark pine
cross-hatching the sliver
of burnished steel.
I don't know whether
to keep trying or turn back,
accept I've glimpsed
that arc of deep water
where ducks take off
in stepped formations,
like porcelain fowl flying
across a suburban wall.

Lake

and even with all the forgiving   the being
in this moment and this   following every
tilt and shift of the world   the stillness of snow
the seeping of grey dawn over the grimy sill
the curdy light of the city and its stale breathing
it's then I think of that dark lake   the trees
leaning out over its black mirrored skin
fringed with purple loosestrife that grows
along the edge of slow moving water
the bulrushes reflected in its anthracite
depths and imagine diving   down and down
into that icy water   through duckweed
and pools of green algae   watermeal
and water hyacinths   milfoil and hydrilla
to be caught in tendrils of curly-leaf pond weed
then on   deeper still   past clasping-leaf
pondweed with its thin and delicate oval
shaped leaves   that are wide and wavy
coontail that lacks any true roots and the naiad
and sago pondweed   to where light ceases
downwards   with this cold seal body
towards that lost thing   that special thing
I know is there in the muddy depths
till I can no longer go on holding my breath

Last Look

The last day at the lake
and the page of dark water
remains inscrutable. Late
summer sun decorates
its untroubled surface
with swirls of September
calligraphy, fallen leaves
bob on the copper swells,
votives to a past summer
that promised so much.
A single moorhen
does what moorhens do.
The breeze is still warm
against hungry skin
but beneath the calm
are depths of black water,
tangles of duckweed
that can pull a swimmer down,
nostrils and lungs
clogging with thick sludge,
the words all drowned.

Return

for Seamus Heaney

His hands grubbed where once his spade
dug potato drills. Not to pick
the black-eyed spuds of boyhood

that on mizzling mornings he gathered
for his father in the old enamel pail —
broken nails crescent-moons of earth,

his carthorse boots heavy with clay —
but to sort vowels and furled consonants
echoing with lost voices and rain.

In ditch and flooded field, he cocked an ear
to the land for sounds of ancient accents
that whispered from the bog like savage prayers.

Now he's slipped away and in the evening wind,
we listen amid shadows of rust for his footfalls,
while beneath the soaking furze,

she waits, the women in a dress of sodden leaves,
that torque of beaten iron about her throat,
a chalice of bone lifted to welcome him home.

Remembering Laugharne

In memory of Dylan Thomas

How odd, after all these years
to return to the boathouse as the dawn mist
rises ghostly as a lapwing's heart-cry

to lure daybreak from the grieving dark,
and catch the ghost of you out on the mudflats
in your old tweed coat

whelking for poems:
my beast, my angel, my fat little fool.
On these tidal reaches

Where Taf, Towy and Gwendraeth
meet and boats lie beached in
a silver throat of brackish water,

I danced barefoot, gathered cockles
in the hem of my long skirt, salty vulvae
to boil in a broth for you on the black iron stove.

At night, in our pink bedroom
you sucked me clean amid a musk
of winter apples, spilt bottles of ale.

Rats scuttled in the privy. Bath time
I'd lay out dolly mixture in the soap tray,
scrub your plump baby's back.

Unruly children we clung together
in an adult world. But with the rage,
the drinking, an innocence was lost.

That morning you lay dying across
an ocean, they strapped me in a straightjacket
for smashing the hospital crucifix.

Still, I see your curly head against
the regulation pillow. Those little
fin-like hands curled on the white sheet.

III

*... not till we have lost the world do we begin to find ourselves,
and realise where we are ...*

Henry David Thoreau

Lost

This is where you've arrived. City of dreams and shadows.
A maze of nameless streets, closed entrance halls and small squares.

Steps of red roof tiles rise on three hills enclosing the suckling she-wolf
inside bastion walls. Loneliness rings from the tongues of the *campanili*.

Swallows swoop at home in their own sky. The light is fading
and bright restaurants fill with lives that are not yours.

Couples kiss in the Piazza del Campo as evening gathers in
a corner of the square. A waiter brings a basket of bread,

a carafe of wine. Desire fills the empty spaces. There's nowhere
to get to anymore so, in arm with what might have been,

you make your *passeggiata*, past courtyards and shuttered windows,
with no way of knowing which direction points home.

Afternoon in Siena

After Cavafy

Soon I will know this room.
It will have become familiar.
Then sometime after I've left
they'll rent it to another writer
or student, a couple on holiday
for a long weekend.
For now, I'll try to fix it in my mind,
this ordinary room with its cold
tile floor without a rug,
the low chair and ugly wardrobe
with its foxed glass,
the shuttered windows that open
onto the narrow street where,
in the evening, a small dog yaps
and yelps beneath the washing line,
the purple canopy of wisteria.
And in the corner, the messy bed,
where in another life
we might have made love —
the afternoon sun
bathing us in liquid light —
if only I knew who you were.

Reading the City

Siena

I scan the street like a page.
What might have been lies in wait for me
somewhere in the heart of this ancient city.
The life of that woman hanging her washing
on the line above the square —
her pink petticoat and green skirt —
that could be mine.
Shadows peel from her face.
Iron balustrades and heavy doors
are scarred by their histories, alleyways
and passages just what they seem.
In the upholsterer's workshop and
bookbinder's studio all is lost in the telling
as forms shift though these dark lanes
without your love.

The weight of history

Good Friday. It's unseasonably cold.
A sharp wind cuts through
the hive of streets.

In the *Pinacoteca Nazionale*
dim rooms overflow with
taciturn Madonnas ascending

to heaven among angelic choirs.
Baby Jesus sits on her lap hunched
beneath his old man's face.

So many saints. So much holiness.
And so much gold.
In the long gallery

I write in my notebook as if
life depends on it. Yet isn't all
language a form of deceit?

Outside the city gathers
in its furtive *contrada*:
the *Tartuca*, the *Civetta*, the *Bruco* —

young men practise
manoeuvres with medieval flags.
With such a weight of history

I hanker for streets littered
with broken glass and beer cans,
eggshells and condoms,

where love is just another word
for heartache
and I feel almost at home.

Santa Maria della Scala

Easter and the museum's empty.
Nothing but relics and saints' bones.
A thumb, a foreskin.

It's impossible to tell,
in their ornate reliquaries, what things are.
And holy of holies, a sacred nail

sits beside a gilded gospel
enamelled in cobalt blue,
where tiny Byzantine figures —

monks and farriers — remain forever
in the 11th century. Once this maze
of crypts housed weary pilgrims.

Wet nurses suckled abandoned infants
for a fee. Its founder — so my Blue Guide
tells me — died in 893. Being here,

certainly, gives you time
to contemplate the brevity of it all.
To wonder where this strip of cloth,

a sliver of the Virgin's belt, has been
these many years and whether
all truth contains a contradiction

so, even though there's no heaven,
I wonder, if I stand here long enough,
I might learn the art of prayer.

Sanctuary House of
St. Catherine of Siena

Easter Sunday.
Alone in this strange city
I'm suddenly aware I'm old.
Not very old
but not young anymore,
which is what I'm used to.
Waking in the pale dawn
believing that tomorrow
will be different from today.
Standing in front of a glass
to paint my lips red
before scanning the crowd
for a face that might mirror
a flicker of desire.
How did it happen that what
I've grown used to should
so sneakily change?
White roses and laurels decorate
St. Catherine's sacred house.
I'd light a candle to us both —
but there's only a row
of cheap electric lights where,
when you place your money
in a slot, a naked bulb
lights up, momentarily.

Bar

Below the church of St. Catherine,
in a side-street bar,
the drinks are cheap and the music loud.

Girls in tight jeans lean into young men
who could be Zeffirelli extras
with their dark halos of curls.

Sitting with my glass of rough red,
watching them smoke and flirt
as evening gathers among

the Campari and neon,
it's easy to imagine my life
just like theirs, mirrored infinitely

in the bar's smeared glass.
Yet when I glance past
the laughter and the smoke rings,

back down the murky alley
the way I just came, I realise
that around the next bend

there's no room waiting filled
with beeswax candles and a crumpled bed,
where muslin curtains lift

in the evening air
and clouds of swallows circle
and circle in the growing dark.

A search for lightness
against the weight of living

fantasy is a place where it rains...

CALVINO

This city without a river refuses to yield up
its past, engraved like lines on an old man's hand.

It's there in the trickle of the tortoise fountain,
the corner of the winding alley where washing

hangs near the synagogue by a pink wall,
in the reflections of the mullioned windows

and peanut seller's stall. Those iron grills
and evening's insistent bell.

Even in the constant rain drip-dripping
from the purple udders of wisteria.

Tomorrow I'll go out and meet myself
in a shop window. Sit in a café

to eat black olives and bread.
Write in my notebook,

for we travel to discover who we are.
But tonight, I'll undo the buttons

of this white blouse, toss it on a chair,
sleep alone beneath these old stars.

Vanishing Point

April morning and out beyond the city
the hills are strung with vineyards,
church towers and rows of cypress trees.
No wilderness of laundrettes or builders' yards
leech from the suburb's ragged edge.
Just a patch of olive in thick strokes
of silvery green. A stone farmhouse nestled
beneath red-scalloped tiles in bold perspective.
It might be a Renaissance painting,
where down in the valley a barefoot
shepherd sits minding his flock,
as a soldier in colourful hose goes riding by.
It's not difficult to believe it's 1553
and that I'm looking out on the world
through a window. Straight down
the road as far as the eye can see,
where parallel lines converge in a single
vanishing point, as if that were the future.

Fishers of Men

After Duccio di Buoninsegna

Raw blue light.
A morning moon and small wind
hold us fast between sea and sky.
Dawn hangs exhausted
above the lake of Tiberiade,
our sails weighed down
with morning dew.
All night we caught nothing,
Our aching bodies pliable
as waves bent beneath
the heavy dark. Wet wood
creaking against worn leather.
Now, dog tired, we wash
our empty nets, though all
we want is a cup of wine,
a dry shirt and bed.
God and miracles are far
from our minds
as we heave in the windlass
just one more time.
In this floating world where
sea is made of words,
waves whisper covenants
and fish become men,
silver bodies spill through
the mesh, fish scales
coating our skin in
shimmering benedictions.

Duccio's Dawn

Day break and a mint light unfurls in the *bottega*'s
dark corners. Between church bell and dog bark
he bends to strengthen seasoned panels of poplar

with strips of linen, size them with rabbit glue
and chalky gesso sanded smooth as a woman's skin.
A reed marks out the ghost of angels,

smudged charcoal is erased with a feather.
With squirrel brush and ink-wash he fills in drapery.
Shadows are applied with something blunter.

And then the gold. Tooled and punched with flowers
and stars. Cusped Gothic arches polished to burn bright
in deep church dark. At last the tempera:

terra verde, orpiment, cinnabar bound
with egg yolk and water that takes years to dry.
Yellow from country fowl for swarthy peasants.

Pale ones from town hens for the blessed saints.
And in the dusty silence he murmurs *credos*,
paternosters, an Ave Maria —

asks the Virgin to infuse his tongue
with that metallic taste of miracles
so he can paint the face of God.

Barreiro

Beneath purple jacarandas young men
gather with old men's faces, tattoos
and bottles of beer. A pack of cigarettes.

Graffiti daubs the walls of the cobbled square.
Balustrades crumble on opera-set houses
where local dignitaries and teachers

once sang *fado* in jasmine-scented air.
Now, wrecked staircases cling for dear life.
Half the buildings are for sale.

Observation: a cluster of plastic bottles
hangs from a lamp post like blossom.
It seems to be art. A lemon light bounces

from the collapsed rooftops. Outside
the dingy café, a young mother's T-shirt
brags in English: 'I'm exactly where I need to be'.
.
Along the Rio Tejo cement works,
ferry termini and warehouses replace
fishing boats and windmills.

Villages die. Towns die. History
is never satisfied. And the similarity
between decay and earthquakes?

The beauty of ruins.
When I look up Barreiro, Trip Advisor
tells me there's nothing to do.

Travelling Alone

From this high kitchen window
I look down on a small suburban square
where old meets new,
nodding like polite acquaintances
lifting their hats in the morning sun:
the concrete mini-market and hair salon,
the Dream Café where, under white umbrellas,
ladies of a certain age chatter over
café pingado and *Pastéis de Nata*.

Last evening, my first,
small patches of yellowing sunlight
netted the park's gravel, its faded grass,
cross-hatching the statue,
the hubbub of children, girls in clusters
wedded to their mobile phones,
old men on benches smoking,
for whom this place is home.

How did I get from there to here?
What route lead me in search
of a heart to call my own?
Though I've wiped shit from babies' bums,
held the frail hands of the dying,
I'm orphaned from myself,
lost in a landscape that despite
endless movement doesn't change.
Voices I don't understand blow in
through the open window.
I pick up my pen and begin to write,
unpacking these words to discover
what I've become.

Night Square

Midnight,
from this kitchen window
I look down like a princess

in her high tower,
onto the empty square,
a stage-set lit

with phosphorus streetlamps,
the flashing green cross
of the pharmacy,

café tables and chairs
neatly stacked as if there's
just been a performance,

white umbrellas
furled like shrouds.
Then out of the shadows

a couple wanders
arm in arm, diagonally,
from the far corner

towards the trees but,
in a moment, are gone,
so all that's left are the flashing

green cross, the stacked chairs
and furled umbrellas, as the night
continues its weary way.

Narrative Grace

How did I find myself here?
  In this place that for others is home.
I've travelled so far, searched high and low,

from distant Kerry shoreline,
  to this cobbled Portuguese square,
through the detritus of Sicilian markets,

to fetid Venetian canals but still
  not found you. If I close my eyes
I can hear your voice. Sonorous, familiar,

droll, as you talk of poetry and art.
  In that blood-red darkness
I can almost taste your salt-licked skin,

touch the ragged ribbon
  of your boyhood scars
that tell me you are real.

How strange I've become to myself
  here in Barreiro,
both citizen and exile.

Yet when the sweet girl with
  the broken tooth brings my *caldo verde*
I feel I almost belong.

Perspective is everything.
  What we come to accept,
a form of narrative grace.

Remembering Pessoa

This town's unknown to me,
the streets new. I forget why
I came here. Yet I could simply
step out of my life like throwing
off an old coat, rent a small room
with hairline cracks across the ceiling,
a desk looking out over the square
where women walk their dogs
and boys play football up
against the rough stone wall.
I could wake each morning
to make coffee on this little stove,
listen to the chirping of the black
Crested Myna birds, the children
on their way to school.
I'd speak to no one.
Just nod at the gap-toothed
girl in the dark café,
who'd nod back
and smile when she bought
my mid-day espresso.
I could borrow another's fears.
Wear them instead of my own.
Exchange old yearnings
for what might have been,
the longed-for loves
that never came my way.
My head aches because
my heart aches, so I write
and write to give meaning
to what isn't there.

Not simply air

All morning the dry *meltemi*
lifts the waves like sneaky Neptune
peering under his daughter's frilled skirts.
I came here to find form and structure,
to feel my feet planted firmly along
the blue earth's spine, toes curled
for balance around it's bony nodules.
Through the wind's fierce hiss
I can hear the Aegean speaking in
its own tongue, indifferent to desire
and history, the fragile longing for
the fingertips of an unknown hand
to brush this salted strand of hair
from my sunburnt cheek
reminding me that I'm not simply air.

Swimming to Albania

At night, the solitary moon
swims outside my window,
phosphorescence spangling her milky skin.
Though she rides and surfs the waves,
carefree as a dolphin, her body
remembers how once blind night
hauled her into its secret bed
feeling beneath her seaweed camisole
with its tongue of shadows.
But for now, she must swim alone,
disorientated beneath the cloudless sky,
while love points its long bone finger
towards the mountains of Albania.

Those Far Blue Hills

I have become a connoisseur of roads,
having grown weary of anticipation,
of waiting too long in the dark hours
for whispered promises and midnight calls.
Now I take this solitary journey
down hidden byways and lanes, hauling this horse-hair body
towards those far blue hills and stagnant dykes,
the shifting sands and impatient cities.
Longing for wilderness I've become a storyteller
of absence and loss, though all travel
is a form of return as well as departure.
Between barren islands and bare rocks
I trek this narrow path without
losing sight of the stony shore,
where a white haar draws in
across the purple sky
and this journey ceases.

SUE HUBBARD is an award-winning poet, novelist, broadcaster and art critic. Twice winner of the London Writers Competition and winner of third prize in the National Poetry Competition, her publications include *Everything Begins with the Skin* (Enitharmon), *Ghost Station* and *The Forgetting and Remembering of Air* (Salt), *The Idea of Islands: a collaboration with the artist Donald Teskey* (Occasional Press, Ireland). Twenty of her poems appeared in *Oxford Poets 2000: an Anthology* (Carcanet) and, as the Poetry Society's only Public Art Poet, she was responsible for London's largest public art poem, *Eurydice*, at Waterloo. Her poems have been read on *Poetry Please*, *The Verb* and *Front Row* and appeared in *The Irish Times*, *The Observer* and numerous magazines and anthologies and have been recorded for the *Poetry Archive*.

Her prose and novels include *Rothko's Red: short stories* (Salt), *Depth of Field* (Dewi Lewis) and *Girl in White* (Cinnamon Press). Her third novel, *Rainsongs*, is published by Duckworth, UK, Overlook Press, US, Mercure de France and Yilin Press, China.

As an art critic she has written regularly for *The Independent*, *The Independent on Sunday*, *Time Out*, *The New Statesman* and many leading art magazines. Her selected art writings *Adventures in Art* is published by Other Criteria.

She has an MA in Creative Writing from the University of East Anglia and twice been a Hawthornden Fellow. In 1999 she was awarded a major Arts Council award to finish her second novel.

Swimming to Albania is her fourth collection.

The Salmon Bookshop
& Literary Centre

Ennistymon, County Clare, Ireland

salmonpoetry

Cliffs of Moher, County Clare, Ireland

"Like the sea-run Steelhead salmon that thrashes upstream to its spawning ground, then instead of dying, returns to the sea—Salmon Poetry Press brings precious cargo to both Ireland and America in the poetry it publishes, then carries that select work to its readership against incalculable odds."

TESS GALLAGHER